CONTENTS

Famous Firsts

1 The first airplane was flown in 1903 by:

- **a** Igor Sikorsky ☐
- **b** Orville Wright ☐
- **c** James Doolittle ☐

2 The first President to serve a third term:

- **a** Woodrow Wilson ☐
- **b** Dwight D. Eisenhower ☐
- **c** Franklin Delano Roosevelt ☐

3 The first meeting of the United Nations General Assembly was held in:

- **a** 1946 ☐
- **b** 1920 ☐
- **c** 1950 ☐

5

4 The first intercollegiate football game in the United States was played in 1869 between:

a Yale and Harvard ☐
b Penn and Cornell ☐
c Rutgers and Princeton ☐

5 The first atomic-powered submarine was launched in 1954 by:

a Russia ☐
b United States ☐
c France ☐

6 The world's first artificial satellite was launched in 1957 by:

   a The United States ☐
   b England ☐
   c Russia ☐

7 The first man to orbit the earth was:

   a Alan Shepard ☐
   b Yuri Gagarin ☐
   c John Glenn ☐

8 The first man to walk on the moon was:

   a Edwin Aldrin ☐
   b Neil Armstrong ☐
   c Michael Collins ☐

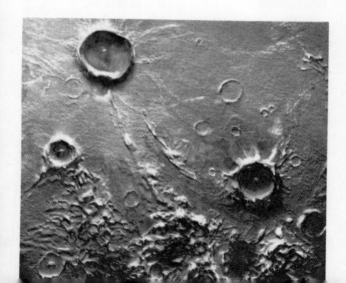

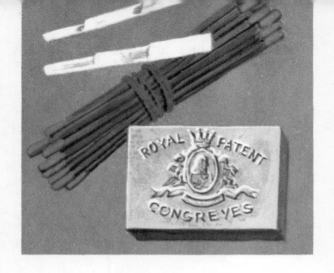

Word Matches

Find the wrong word in each sentence, and replace it with the correct word from the list below.

a delegate
b cosmic
c distinguished
d fragrant
e corps
f junction

g irritation
h launch
i congratulate
j aspires
k larynx
l entertain

1 Today they are going to lance the ship.

2 She lives at the junket of Fourth and Broadway.

3 He is in the officers' training corpse.

---

4 The rejected applicant tried to conceal his irrigation.

---

5 Every delicate to the conference will be heard.

---

6 Astronauts will have to guard against cosmetic rays.

---

7 I want to congregate you on your promotion.

---

8 Roses are very fragment flowers.

---

9 Our principal is a very extinguished man.

---

10 She inspires to be an actress.

---

11 I will now ascertain you with a new card trick.

---

12 I have a cold in my lynx.

For Bird Watchers

1 What bird can fly up and down, sideways and backward?

---

2 What American bird lays its egg in the nests of other birds, leaving the care of the young to the birds that made the nest?

---

3 What bird is the national emblem of the United States?

---

4 What birds can walk under water in a stream?

---

5 What birds often weave a cast-off snake skin into their nests?

---

6 What bird opens clams by dropping them from the air onto a hard surface?

---

7 What birds hide worms for use in winter weather?

---

8 What birds carry messages for men?

---

9 What is the smallest bird in the world?

10 What bird family is the largest in the world?

11 What bird can fly the fastest?

12 What are the largest flying birds?

About the United States

1 What was the first university to be founded on the North American continent?

   a Yale ☐
   b Harvard ☐
   c Princeton ☐

2 How long are flags flown at half mast on the death of a President?

   a 30 days ☐
   b one day ☐
   c six months ☐

3 The lowest geographical point in the United States is 242 feet below sea level. Where is it?

   a Long Island, New York ☐
   b Death Valley, California ☐
   c Savannah, Georgia ☐

4 What is the national anthem of the United States?

   a The Battle Hymn of the Republic ☐
   b American the Beautiful ☐
   c The Star-Spangled Banner ☐

5 The Continental Divide is:

a a high ridge running through the Rocky Mountains ☐
b a bridge which divides the eastern and western parts of the U.S. ☐
c the river which separates Texas from Mexico ☐

6 The highest mountain in the United States is 20,320 feet high. It is:

a Mt. Everest ☐
b North Peak ☐
c Mt. McKinley ☐

7 Over one thousand species of trees are found in the United States. How much of the United States is forest land?

a Nearly one-third ☐
b Over one-half ☐
c One-eighth ☐

8 The Statue of Liberty is 152 feet high and stands in New York Harbor. It was:

a built by Chinese immigrants ☐
b erected by the United States Government ☐
c presented to the American people by France ☐

9 Niagara Falls is 167 feet in height. Among the world's highest waterfalls, it ranks:

  a 7th ☐
  b 21st ☐
  c 49th ☐

10 A part of the United States borders on the second largest lake in the world. Can you name the lake?

  a Lake Michigan ☐
  b Lake Huron ☐
  c Lake Superior ☐

Adam to Zechariah

The questions in this quiz are based
on stories from the Old Testament.

1 How long did it take God to create the
world, according to the Book of Genesis?

   a six years ☐
   b six centuries ☐
   c six days ☐

2 The Old Testament says that God created Adam in His own image and likeness. How was Eve created?

   a from the limb of a tree ☐
   b from an apple ☐
   c from Adams' rib ☐

3 Who lost his life after being tricked into having his hair cut?

   a David ☐
   b Jason ☐
   c Samson ☐

4 Who wore a coat of many colors when he was sold into slavery by his brothers?

   a Joseph ☐
   b Haman ☐
   c Shadrack ☐

5 What caused the walls of Jericho to crumble?

   a blasts from trumpets ☐
   b battering rams ☐
   c a violent earthquake ☐

6 Who was found in a basket in the bulrushes?

   a Abel ☐
   b Moses ☐
   c the Pharaoh's daughter ☐

7 Goliath was killed by David with:

   a an arrow ☐
   b a stone from a sling ☐
   c a dagger ☐

8 Who commanded the Israelite army at the Battle of Jericho?

   a Jeremiah ☐
   b Caesar ☐
   c Joshua ☐

9 What happened to the Pharaoh's army when it pursued the Jews on their flight from captivity in Egypt?

    a they were drowned ☐
    b they were lost in the desert ☐
    c they were turned to stone ☐

10 Who came out alive from the stomach of a whale?

    a Jacob ☐
    b Jonah ☐
    c Joseph ☐

11 With what Old Testament personage do we connect the word *patience?*

    a Adam ☐
    b Job ☐
    c David ☐

12 Who in the Old testament was renowned for his wisdom?

    a Joshua ☐
    b Solomon ☐
    c Daniel ☐

Science and Invention

1 The ancient Greeks thought that there were only four basic elements. Two of these were Earth and Air. What do you suppose the other two were?

_____

2 In what field of science were the ancient Greeks most interested?

_____

3 Where did the first man-made atomic reaction take place and who was responsible for it?

_____

4 When it was launched, the submarine _Nautilus_ was different from any other vessel in the world. What made it different?

_____

5 The scientist who invented the phonograph was the same man who gave the world the incandescent light bulb. What was his name?

_____

6 Why can a bird alight on a high-voltage wire without being electrocuted?

_____

7 Which of the following will *not* conduct electricity; water, silver, aluminum, wood, rubber, copper?

_____

8 Which of the following use electricity as their power source: automobile, subway train, diesel locomotive, jet plane, TV set?

_____

Vis-à-Vis

Here are some familiar foreign words and phrases.
Select the correct meaning for each.

1 au courant   **a** with currants ☐
                  b well-informed ☐

2 anno Domini   **a** at an advanced age ☐
                  b in the year of our Lord ☐

3 à votre santé   **a** to your health ☐
                  b be sure to vote ☐

4 alfresco   **a** fresh eggs ☐
                  b out of doors ☐

5 au contraire   **a** for my country ☐
                  b on the contrary ☐

6 divide et impera   **a** divide and rule ☐

                        b a balanced scale ☐

7 poco a poco   **a** politely ☐

                        b little by little ☐

8 e pluribus unum   **a** one out of many ☐

                        b a happy marriage ☐

9 cause célèbre   **a** a famous person ☐

                        b a famous legal case ☐

10 lieder   **a** a political leader ☐

                        b a group of songs ☐

11 Deo gratias   **a** on a fine day ☐

                        b thanks be to God ☐

12 nom de plume   **a** a pen name ☐

                        b a feathered hat ☐

13 vis-à-vis   **a** face to face ☐

                        b neck and neck ☐

14 quid pro quo   **a** something queer ☐

                        b tit for tat ☐

15 à la mode   **a** served with ice cream ☐

                        b imitating the French ☐

Politics

1 The two major political parties in the U.S. are the Republican and the Democrat. The two major political parties in England are:

    a Socialist and Communist ☐
    b Conservative and Labour ☐
    c Federalist and Whig ☐

2 Headquarters of one of the most important international organizations is located in New York City. It is:

    a The United Nations ☐
    b NATO ☐
    c International Red Cross ☐

3 The revolution fought for "Liberty, Equality, and Fraternity" was the:

  a French Revolution ☐
  b American Revolution ☐
  c Glorious Revolution ☐

4 Yugoslavia and Rumania are countries in Eastern Europe. Which one of the following countries is also in Eastern Europe?

  a Italy ☐
  b Sweden ☐
  c Czechoslovakia ☐

5 Southeast Asia has been in the news because of the Vietnam war. If you were to visit this area, which one of the following countries would you include?

  a China ☐
  b Laos ☐
  c Afghanistan ☐

6 Apartheid is a racial segregation policy practiced in:

  a the Republic of South Africa ☐
  b the United States ☐
  c the United Arab Republic ☐

Colorful Places

How's your geography? Match the correct
place names with the descriptions below.

a White Plains
b The Black Forest
c The Blue Ridge
d The Coral Sea
e Orange
f The Golden Gate
g The White Sea
h The Green
  Mountains
i The Red Sea
j The Gold Coast

k The Black Hills
l White Sands
m Greenland
n The Black Sea
o Ivory Coast
p The White
  Mountains
q The Red River
r Yellowstone
s The Orange River
t Green Bay

1 A coastal area of West Africa,
  now Ghana, an independent state ____
2 On the West coast of Africa ____
3 A sea between Arabia and Africa
4 City in Wisconsin ____
5 In Vermont ____
6 A river in South Africa ____
7 A national park in Wyoming ____
8 In the Soviet Union ____
9 A sea between Europe and Asia ____

In the Swim

Match the descriptions below with the
slang phrases on the opposite page.

a At a time of need

b Almost accomplished

c Left in the lurch

d Having inside information

e Not knowing

f Back in the hills

g Not guilty

h In debt

i Go to bed

j Having social connections

k Now being produced

l Be a failure

m	In very good health	**q**	Stopped before it happens
n	In jail	**r**	Rich
o	In trouble	**s**	Rumored
p	Foretold	**t**	Seeking election

1 In the bag   ____
2 Nipped in the bud   ____
3 In the cards   ____
4 In the chips   ____
5 In the clear   ____
6 In the clink   ____
7 In the dark   ____
8 In hot water   ____
9 Hit the hay   ____
10 In the know   ____
11 Holding the bag   ____
12 In the ring   ____
13 Lay an egg   ____
14 In the pink   ____
15 In the red   ____
16 In a pinch   ____
17 In the sticks   ____
18 In the swim   ____
19 In the wind   ____
20 In the works   ____

Little Tests

Match the storybook characters below
with their descriptions.

a Ten Little Indians
b Little Boy Blue
c The Little Match Girl
d Little Tommy Tucker
e Little Jack Horner
f Little Red Riding Hood
g Little Orphan Annie
h Chicken Little
i Little Bo-Peep
j The Little Red Hen
k Little Miss Muffet
l Little John

1 She sat on the grass to eat. _____
2 He sat in a corner to eat. _____
3 He performed for his dinner. _____
4 He was a young man with a horn. _____
5 There were 10 at the beginning
and 1 at the end. _____
6 She used up what she was selling,
to keep warm. _____
7 She could hardly recognize
her old grandma. _____

8 She would be a failure
on a sheep ranch.   ____

9 She's a comic strip character
whose best friend is a dog.   ____

10 He was a "strong-arm" man
in Sherwood Forest.   ____

11 She made a loaf of bread and
wouldn't let anyone else eat it.   ____

12 She thought the sky
was falling down.   ____

Facts about Animals

1 Name the world's largest animal.

---

2 Camels and lions have been known to live for forty years or more, but one animal has been known to live as long as 177 years. Do you know which animal?

---

3 What does a camel store in his hump?

---

4 Race horses can run about forty miles per hour but there is one animal which has been clocked at seventy miles per hour. Can you name it?

5 What fish shoot their prey by hitting them with drops of water squirted forcefully from their mouth?

6 Name at least three other animals besides the cow whose milk is used as human food in various parts of the world.

7 The largest of all living birds is so heavy that it cannot fly. What is it?

8 The anaconda is one of the largest and most deadly of constricting snakes. Where is it found?

9 What is the rhinoceros' horn made of?

33

10 Name the largest and most ferocious of the killer dinosaurs.

_____

11 Which animal is known as the King of Beasts?

_____

12 How many stomachs does a cow have?

_____

13 What is a marsupial?

_____

14 What animal will help another female of the same species raise her young?

_____

15 Why do whales spout?

_____

34

John Brown
and Other Johns

The name John appears in many languages
in various forms. In French it is *Jean,* and in Spanish,
Juan. The nickname for John, as you probably know,
is Jack. These questions are about various Johns.

1 The man who became president upon the
death of Lincoln was:

   a John Tyler   ☐
   b Andrew Johnson   ☐
   c Lyndon Johnson   ☐

2 The nickname of John Chapman, the
American folk hero who planted apple seeds
was:

   a Johnny Applehead   ☐
   b Johnny Appleseed   ☐
   c Johnny Appletree   ☐

3 The anti-slavery crusader who raided
the arsenal at Harpers Ferry, Va., just before the Civil War was:

   a Jean Valjean   ☐
   b Don Juan   ☐
   c John Brown   ☐

4 In 1215 King John of England was forced by the aristocracy to sign a document limiting the powers of the King. This historical document is known as:

   a the Emancipation Proclamation ☐
   b the Magna Carta ☐
   c the Bill of Rights ☐

5 A naval hero of the American Revolution who cried, "I have not yet begun to fight!" was:

   a John J. Pershing ☐
   b John Paul Jones ☐
   c John Stuart Mill ☐

6 John Wilkes Booth was a member of a famous theatrical family. He was also:

   a the man who killed Alexander Hamilton in a duel ☐
   b a Shakespearean actor ☐
   c the actor who assassinated President Lincoln ☐

7 Who holds the record for being the first man to high jump more than seven feet?

   a John Thomas ☐
   b John Fromm ☐
   c John Olson ☐

8 An early American family gave the United States two presidents, both named John. The family name is:

   a Adams ☐
   b Davis ☐
   c Brooks ☐

9 A famous American band leader and composer of many popular marches was:

   a John Coltrane ☐
   b John Jacob Astor ☐
   c John Philip Sousa ☐

Top This One

Which of these "top" words fits
the descriptions below?

a topcoat   **f** topmost

b topsoil   **g** topsail

c top-heavy   **h** carrot top

d topknot   **i** topnotch

e topsy-turvy   **j** top hat

1 A person with red hair is
often called   ____

2 When something is really the best
in its field, we say that it is   ____

3 When things are in a state of
confusion, we might say they are   ____

4 A lightweight outer garment is a   ____

5 A formal head covering
for men is a   ____

6 The surface layer of earth
in your garden is   ____

7 One of the sails on a boat is the   ____

8 If your mother puts up her hair,
she may have a   ____

9 If you drop an armful of things,
it may have been because
your load was   ____

10 The highest rung on the
ladder is   ____

Sports and Sportsmen

1 Who was the first baseball player to hit more than 60 home runs in one season?

---

2 The greatest all-around woman athlete of all time is generally considered to have been?

---

3 In professional football, what city do the Packers represent?

---

4 In what sport is the Masters Tournament an important event?

5 What sport is played on ponies, with mallets?

---

6 In what city and state is the Rose Bowl located?

---

7 In professional basketball, what city do the Royals represent?

---

8 Who was the first Negro woman to win the Winbledon and United States tennis championships?

---

9 Baseball is said to be the national pastime of the United States. What sport is the national pastime of many countries in Europe, South America, and Africa?

---

10 Jesse Owens is considered by many to be one of the greatest track performers of all time. At the 1936 Olympics, how many gold medals did he win?

---

11 What sport do you think of when America's Cup is mentioned?

---

12 What college football team is nicknamed "The Fighting Irish"?

---

13 Phil Hill and Stirling Moss are famous for excellence in what sport?

---

14 In what sport are these terms familiar: blue line, puck, penalty box?

---

15 With what sport are these terms associated: épée, foil, saber?

What Is It?

1 An Arctic Tern   _____
2 A German Shepherd   _____
3 A Koala Bear   _____
4 A Praying Mantis   _____
5 A Red Admiral   _____
6 A Plymouth Rock   _____
7 A Devil Ray   _____
8 A Virginia Creeper   _____
9 A Gila Monster   _____
10 A Peacemaker   _____
11 A New York Giant   _____

Select from:

a A sticklike insect
b A climbing garden vine
c A furry Australian animal
d A migratory sea bird
e A poisonous lizard
f A professional football player
g A bat-like marine animal
h A species of butterfly
i A breed of chicken
j A Western handgun
k A large watchdog

Who's Zoo?

None of these interesting creatures can be found
in the zoo, yet all should be as familiar as
a SACRED COW or a COLD FISH.

It means: Its initials are:

1 A family outcast   B _____   S _____

2 A constant reader   B _____   W _____

3 A miser   C _____   S _____

4 An imitator   C _____   C _____

5 A long-shot candidate   D _____   H _____

6 A simple soul   D _____   B _____

7 A glutton for work   E _____   B _____

8 First to arrive   E _____   B _____

9 A late-late show watcher N _____   O _____

10 An active worker   B _____   B _____

11 A solitary operator   L _____   W _____

12 An easy target   S _____   D _____

43

Military History

1 The Napoleonic Wars lasted for nearly 20 years. Napoleon was finally defeated in:

a The Battle of Elba ☐
b The Battle of Waterloo ☐
c The Battle of Austerlitz ☐

2 During the Revolutionary War, a certain American officer was known as the Swamp Fox, because of his bold raids against the British in the swampy regions of North Carolina. He was:

a Horatio Gates ☐
b Nathaniel Green ☐
c Francis Marion ☐

3 An American general during the Revolutionary War tried to barter West Point to the British for his own gain—a plan which was unsuccessful. He was:

a John Andre ☐
b Benedict Arnold ☐
c John Burgoyne ☐

4 The first battle of the Revolutionary War was fought on April 19, 1775. The treaty ending the war was signed in:

a 1776 ☐
b 1780 ☐
c 1783 ☐

5 The Union Commander at the Battle of Gettysburg during the Civil War was:

- **a** General Meade ☐
- **b** General Grant ☐
- **c** General Sherman ☐

6 General George Custer was killed in the Battle of Little Big Horn by:

- **a** Confederate troops ☐
- **b** Mexican forces ☐
- **c** Sioux Indians ☐

7 During World War I, a German submarine sank a British liner and nearly 1,200 passengers were lost, including over 100 Americans. The ship was:

- **a** the Lusitania ☐
- **b** the Titanic ☐
- **c** the Stockholm ☐

8 World War I was finally ended when an armistice was signed by the Allies and Germany on:

- **a** November 11, 1918 ☐
- **b** October 31, 1920 ☐
- **c** October 24, 1929 ☐

9 What country did Germany attack and invade to signal the start of World War II?

   a Britain ☐
   b France ☐
   c Poland ☐

10 The Japanese struck at United States military bases on December 7, 1941, bringing the United States into World War II. The Hawaiian base attacked was:

   a Waikiki Beach ☐
   b Diamond Head ☐
   c Pearl Harbor ☐

For the Birds

1 The first powered flight took place in 1903 at:

   a Eagle Rock ☐
   b Ravenswood ☐
   c Kitty Hawk ☐

2 A household songbird named after a group of islands off the coast of Africa is the:

   a parakeet ☐
   b toucan ☐
   c canary ☐

3 Song and legend have told of the beautiful song of:

   a the canary ☐
   b the nightingale ☐
   c the golden eagle ☐

4 Charles Lindberg was nicknamed:

   a The Lone Eagle ☐
   b The Sea Hawk ☐
   c The Sky Falcon ☐

5 "Birdie in the cage" is an expression used by:

    a zoo keepers ☐
    b poultry packers ☐
    c square dance callers ☐

6 A vain person is sometimes said to be "proud as a _____."

    a rooster ☐
    b peacock ☐
    c swan ☐

7 A mythological animal, half lion and half eagle, is called:

   a a griffin ☐
   b a triton ☐
   c a unicorn ☐

8 What bird in a nursery rhyme was killed by a sparrow with an old-fashioned weapon?

   a Cock Robin ☐
   b Goosey Gander ☐
   c Chicken Little ☐

9 What country has the same name as a bird?

   a Lebanon ☐
   b Turkey ☐
   c Pakistan ☐

10 The familiar term "ugly duckling" comes from:

   a the fact that young ducks are so ungainly ☐
   b a famous story by Hans Christian Andersen ☐
   c Dickens' *Oliver Twist* ☐

Double Trouble

Answers will all be words
of two identical syllables, such as **dum-dum.**

1 A native drum beaten by hand

_____

2 Famous little girl comic strip character

_____

3 French sugar candy

_____

4 Mustard pickles

_____

5 What baby brother calls his toy train

_____

6 This skill toy has a string attached to it

_____

7 Just average

_____

8 So long!

_____

9 A doll often says this when picked up
or bent over

_____

10 What a cheerleader might say to spur
her team to victory

_____

"Fee, Fi, Fo, Fum!"

If you read many fairy tales you should
be able to recall these characters.

1 Who got so hopping mad that he went
through the floor and was never seen again?

---

2 In what story did the kiss of a prince
undo the spell of a poisoned apple?

---

3 Which of his mother's prized possessions did Jack trade to a peddler for some magic beans?

---

4 In what story was an emperor fooled by some crafty tailors?

---

5 How did Rapunzel's suitor manage to climb to her balcony?

---

6 Name a tiny person no bigger than your thumb.

---

7 What brother and sister were caught by a hungry witch who lived in a house made of sweets?

---

8 Who was chased by three bears after she ate all the porridge?

---

9 Who wore boots that allowed him to travel seven leagues in one stride?

---

10 Whose grandmother had such big eyes?

Ancient and Primitive Man

1 The study of primitive man is called:

  a anthropology ☐
  b geology ☐
  c philosophy ☐

2 The oldest stage of man's culture is called:

  a the Primitive Age ☐
  b the Old Stone Age ☐
  c the Primeval Age ☐

3 The idea that a royal family descended directly from the gods survived until modern times in:

  a England ☐
  b Israel ☐
  c Japan ☐

4 A Stone Age culture still exists today, composed of people who were completely isolated from the rest of mankind until 1949. They are:

  a the Etruscans ☐
  b the Caribou Eskimos ☐
  c the Aztec Indians ☐

5 Some of man's inventions during the Middle Stone Age when he came out of his cave and became more active were:

    a the canoe, sled, skis   ☐
    b the saddle, bridle, reins   ☐
    c paper, ink, pens   ☐

6 The first true alphabet was developed around 1000 B.C. by:

    a the Greeks   ☐
    b the Phoenicians   ☐
    c the Spartans   ☐

Win, Place or Show

Supply the missing words.

1 _____, Vegetable, and _____

2 _____, Borrow, or _____

3 _____, Book, and Candle

4 _____, Clothing, and Shelter

5 _____, Line, and _____

6 Liberty, _____, Fraternity

56

7 Morning, _____, and _____

8 _____, Stock, and _____

9 _____, Feminine, and _____

10 Past, _____, and _____

11 _____, Look, and _____

12 _____, Writing, and _____

13 _____, Willing, and Able

14 Length, Width, and _____

15 _____, Sea, and _____

16 _____, Dime, and _____

17 Red, _____, and _____

18 Blood, Sweat, and _____

19 _____, Saw, Conquered

20 _____, Fork, and _____

Just Say "Ah"

1 The system that transports blood through the body is called:

- **a** the vegetal system ☐
- **b** the circulatory system ☐
- **c** the endocrine system ☐

2 The body organs concerned with breathing are called collectively:

- **a** the inflationary system ☐
- **b** the pneumatic system ☐
- **c** the respiratory system ☐

3 Messages from the brain are carried to other parts of the body by the:

a esophagus ☐
b spinal cord ☐
c lateral arch ☐

4 The organ which affects the sense of balance is located:

a in the stomach ☐
b in the ear ☐
c in the mouth ☐

5 When a doctor tells you that he will have to remove your appendix, on what part of you will he operate?

a the brain ☐
b the abdomen ☐
c the chest ☐

6 The cells of the blood which destroy bacteria in the body are:

a red corpuscles ☐
b white corpuscles ☐
c nerves ☐

7 The humerus bone is:

    a in the leg □
    b in the arm □
    c in the skull □

8 The human heart is:
    a a gland □
    b a muscle □
    c a tube □

9 What is the average normal body temperature of human beings?

    a 98.6°F. □
    b 93.4°F. □
    c 100.6°F. □

10 How many bones are in the human body?

    a 110 □
    b 206 □
    c 56 □

11 The body of an average man contains approximately how much blood?

    a 12 pints □
    b 4 pints □
    c 20 pints □

Where in the U.S.A.?

1 The state largest in area has the smallest number of people. Which is it?

---

2 The capital of Rhode Island was named by the Puritans. What is it called?

---

3 The stately home of George Washington, in Virginia, is called what?

---

4 What city in the United States makes more automobiles than any other city in the world?

___

5 In which state were the most presidents born?

___

6 The Soap Box Derby is held each year in what Ohio city?

___

7 Two of our states got their names from an Indian tribe that once lived on the western plain. Which two states?

___

8 The capital of Nebraska, which was admitted to the Union after the Civil War, was named after a president. Which president was it?

___

9 To what rock in Massachusetts do many Americans make pilgrimages?

___

10 Which of our states is made up of twenty islands?

___

Are You a Good Mixer?

Match the famous persons with their correct descriptions.

1 Edgar Allan Poe   _____
2 John Philip Sousa   _____
3 Harriet Beecher Stowe   _____
4 Johann Sebastian Bach   _____
5 Woodrow Wilson   _____
6 Ulysses S. Grant   _____
7 Charles A. Lindberg   _____
8 Pablo Picasso   _____
9 Francis Scott Key   _____
10 J. Edgar Hoover   _____
11 William Frederick Cody   _____

a Civil war general, later U.S. President
b German composer
c American aviator
d Author of "The Star-Spangled Banner"
e American bandmaster and composer
f Poet who wrote "The Raven"
g Author of *Uncle Tom's Cabin*
h President during World War I
i American scout nicknamed "Buffalo Bill"
j Modern painter, born in Spain
k Long-time head of the F.B.I.

The Animal World

1 A large animal that once roamed the American plains in vast herds was almost killed off by hunters. It is now protected by the United States government. It is the:

a Wild Ox ☐
b American Bison ☐
c Water Buffalo ☐

2 The panda looks like a teddy bear and acts like a clown. Even though it resembles a bear it is more closely related to the:

a raccoon ☐
b cat ☐
c dog ☐

3 A mammal about the size of a large cat has young that stay in a pouch until about a quarter grown. When cornered, this animal often feigns death. It is:

a a raccoon □
b an oppossum □
c a gopher □

4 Young lions play and purr like large kittens, but tend to become savage as they grow older. They are called:

a kittens □
b cubs □
c pups □

5 Giraffes are the world's tallest animals and may stand as high as:

a 12 feet ☐
b 15 feet ☐
c 18 feet ☐

6 A small animal, similar to a weasel, fearlessly attacks and kills the most poisonous snakes. A native of India, it is:

a a marmoset ☐
b a mongoose ☐
c a baboon ☐

7 Gnus live in African grass country. Dutch settlers called them Wildebeests. They are members of which family?

a antelope ☐
b buffalo ☐
c cattle ☐

8 A male walrus weighs as much as a ton. He is a member of which family?

a seal ☐
b elephant ☐
c whale ☐

9 Beavers are the best engineers of the animal world. They fell trees with their chisel-like teeth and use them to build their homes. These dwellings are known as:

- **a** lodges ☐
- **b** tepees ☐
- **c** pueblos ☐

10 The giraffe has only one relative. It is about the size of a stag and wanders by night in the forest of the Congo. It is:

- **a** a yak ☐
- **b** an okapi ☐
- **c** a llama ☐

Word Search

Replace each word in darker type with its synonym from the list below.

Include   Inflate   Induce   Intrude
Infer   Inspire   Inform   Inspect
Insist   Intend   Intern   Involve

1 The hotel's prices **cover** the cost of meals.

2 I don't want to **interrupt,** but may I come in?

3 It is unfair of you to **demand** that we attend the meeting.

4 The balloon is made of a material which is easy to **expand.**

5 Only a great love of music could **stimulate** a man to write such works.

6 I **plan** to make sure that this unfortunate event does not recur.

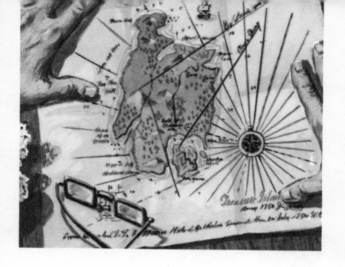

7 Nothing could **persuade** him to go.

8 Am I to **suppose** that you were only playing a joke?

9 We are happy to **tell** you that you have passed the examination.

10 The young doctor will **serve** at the municipal hospital.

11 Don't **entangle** me in your problems.

12 The mechanic will **examine** the car.

What's in a Name?

Many early Anglo-Saxon family names
were once associated with a trade or profession.
See if you can choose the correct meaning
for each name below.

1 Prentice

   a an apprentice

   b a farm hand

   c a house painter

2 Miller

   a a student of moths

   b a long-distance runner

   c a mill keeper

3 Thatcher

    a a wig maker ☐
    b a roofer who uses straw ☐
    c a breeder of ponies ☐

4 Smith

    a a wine merchant ☐
    b a scholar ☐
    c a metal worker ☐

5 Clark

    a a time keeper ☐
    b a spool maker ☐
    c a bookkeeper or clerk ☐

71

6 Steward

  a a cavalier ☐
  b a money lender ☐
  c a gamekeeper or warden ☐

7 Draper

  a a maker of cloth ☐
  b a writer ☐
  c a puppet-maker ☐

8 Cooper

  a a minstrel or bard ☐
  b a miner ☐
  c a barrel maker ☐

9 Mason

  a an engraver ☐
  b an explorer ☐
  c a stone or brick worker ☐

10 Tanner

  a a truant officer ☐
  b a dresser of animal hides ☐
  c an accountant ☐

A Capital Quiz

1 The capital of Japan is:

    a Hiroshima   ☐
    b Tokyo   ☐
    c Yokohama   ☐

2 The capital of Russia is:

    a Leningrad   ☐
    b Kiev   ☐
    c Moscow   ☐

3 The capital of Italy is:

    a Milan   ☐
    b Rome   ☐
    c Naples   ☐

4 The capital of Australia is:

   a Sydney ☐
   b Melbourne ☐
   c Canberra ☐

5 The capital of Canada is:

   a Quebec ☐
   b Montreal ☐
   c Ottawa ☐

6 The capital of India is:

   a New Delhi ☐
   b Bombay ☐
   c Calcutta ☐

7 The capital of Brazil is:

   a Rio de Janeiro ☐
   b Brasilia ☐
   c São Paulo ☐

8 The capital of Spain is:

   a Madrid ☐
   b Barcelona ☐
   c Seville ☐

9 The capital of Israel is:

  a Tel Aviv   ☐

  b Haifa   ☐

  c Jerusalem   ☐

10 The capital of France is:

  a Marseilles   ☐

  b Paris   ☐

  c Bordeaux   ☐

ANSWERS

Famous Firsts (page 5)

1. b: Orville Wright **2.** c: Franklin Delano Roosevelt **3.** a: 1946
4. c: Rutgers and Princeton **5.** b: United States **6.** c: Russia **7.** b:
Yuri Gagarin, a Russian (The first American to orbit the earth
was John Glenn.) **8.** b: Neil Armstrong (July 20, 1969)

Word Matches (page 8)

1. h: launch (not lance) **2.** f: junction (not junket) **3.** e: corps
(not corpse) **4.** g: irritation (not irrigation) **5.** a: delegate (not
delicate) **6.** b: cosmic (not cosmetic) **7.** i: congratulate (not
congregate) **8.** d: fragrant (not fragment) **9.** c: distinguished (not
extinguished) **10.** j: aspires (not inspires) **11.** l: entertain (not
ascertain) **12.** k: larynx (not lynx)

For Bird Watchers (page 10)

1. The Hummingbird **2.** Cowbird **3.** The Bald Eagle, now in danger
of becoming extinct **4.** The Dippers **5.** The Crested Flycatchers
6. Herring Gull **7.** The Jogs **8.** Pigeons **9.** The 2½-inch Bee Hummingbird of the Tropics **10.** The sparrow family, with almost
700 species **11.** The Asian Swift (some timed at 170 mph.) **12.**
California Condor and South American Condor

About the United States (page 12)

1. b: Harvard, in 1636 **2.** a: 30 days **3.** b: Death Valley, California **4.** c: The Star-Spangled Banner **5.** a: a high ridge running
through the Rocky Mountains **6.** c: Mt. McKinley (in Alaska)
7. a: Nearly one-third **8.** c: presented to the American people by
France **9.** c: 49th **10.** c: Lake Superior

Adam to Zechariah (page 16)

1. c: six days (on the seventh day, He rested) **2.** c: from Adam's
rib **3.** c: Samson **4.** a: Joseph **5.** a: blasts from trumpets **6.** b:
Moses **7.** b: a stone from a sling **8.** c: Joshua **9.** a: they were
drowned (After the Israelites had crossed the Red Sea, which
God had parted for them, the Pharaoh's army tried to cross
and the sea closed over them.) **10.** b: Jonah **11.** b: Job **12.** b:
Solomon

Science and Invention (page 20)

1. Fire and Water **2.** Mathematics **3.** At the University of Chi-
cago; Enrico Fermi (Dec. 2, 1942) **4.** It was the first atomic-

powered ship in the world. **5.** Thomas Alva Edison **6.** The bird is not connected to either the ground or another wire; therefore the electricity will not flow through its body. **7.** Rubber and wood will not conduct electricity. **8.** TV set and subway train

Vis-à-Vis (page 22)

1. b: well-informed (French) **2.** b: in the year of our Lord (Latin) **3.** a: to your health (French) **4.** b: out of doors (Italian) **5.** b: on the contrary (French) **6.** a: divide and rule (Latin) **7.** b: little by little (Italian) **8.** a: one out of many (Latin) **9.** b: a famous legal case (French) **10.** b: a group of songs (German) **11.** b: thanks be to God (Latin) **12.** a: a pen name (French) **13.** a: face to face (French) **14.** b: tit for tat (Latin) **15:** a: served with ice cream (French)

Politics (page 24)

1. b: Conservative and Labour **2.** a: The United Nations **3.** a: French Revolution **4.** c: Czechoslovakia **5.** b: Laos **6.** a: the Republic of South Africa

Colorful Places (page 26)

1. j: The Gold Coast **2.** o: Ivory Coast **3.** i: The Red Sea **4.** t: Green Bay **5.** h: The Green Mountains **6.** s: The Orange River **7.** r: Yellowstone **8.** g: The White Sea **9.** n: The Black Sea **10.** b: The Black Forest **11.** d: The Coral Sea **12.** q: The Red River **13.** m: Greenland **14.** p: The White Mountains **15.** l: White Sands **16.** a: White Plains **17.** f: The Golden Gate **18.** c: The Blue Ridge **19.** e: Orange **20.** k: The Black Hills

In the Swim (page 28)

1. b: Almost accomplished **2.** q: Stopped before it happens **3.** p: Foretold **4.** r: Rich **5.** g: Not guilty **6.** n: In jail **7.** e: Not knowing **8.** o: In trouble **9.** i: Go to bed **10.** d: Having inside information **11.** c: Left in the lurch **12.** t: Seeking election **13.** l: Be a failure **14.** m: In very good health **15.** h: In debt **16.** a: At a time of need **17.** f: Back in the hills **18.** j: Having social connections **19.** s: Rumored **20.** k: Now being produced

Little Tests (page 30)

1. k: Little Miss Muffet **2.** e: Little Jack Horner **3.** d: Little Tommy Tucker **4.** b: Little Boy Blue **5.** a: Ten Little Indians **6.** c: The Little Match Girl **7.** f: Little Red Riding Hood **8.** i: Little Bo-Peep **9.** g: Little Orphan Annie **10.** l: Little John **11.** j: The Little Red Hen **12.** h: Chicken Little

Facts about Animals (page 32)

1. The Blue Whale **2.** The Galapagos Tortoise **3.** Fat (his stomach is his water reservoir) **4.** The Cheetah **5.** The Archer Fish **6.** Sheep, Goat, Reindeer, Yak, Musk Ox, Camel, Water Buffalo **7.** The Ostrich **8.** South America **9.** Hair **10.** Tyrannosaurus Rex **11.** The Lion **12.** Four **13.** An animal which carries its newborn young in a pouch. The kangaroo is a marsupial. **14.** Elephants (the helpers are called aunts), and giraffes (the helpers are called nurses) **15.** When a whale rises to the surface, it exhales the air from its lungs. This turns to vapor upon contact with the cooler air. This vapor jet is the familiar spout.

John Brown and Other Johns (page 35)

1. b: Andrew Johnson **2.** b: Johnny Appleseed **3.** c: John Brown **4.** b: the Magna Carta **5.** b: John Paul Jones **6.** c: the actor who assassinated President Lincoln **7.** a: John Thomas (an American) **8.** a: Adams (John Adams and his son John Quincy Adams, the second and the sixth United States presidents) **9.** c: John Philip Sousa

Top This One (page 38)

1. h: carrot top **2.** i: topnotch **3.** e: topsy-turvy **4.** a: topcoat **5.** j: top hat **6.** b: topsoil **7.** g: topsail **8.** d: topknot **9.** c: top-heavy **10.** f: topmost

Sports and Sportsmen (page 39)

1. Roger Maris, New York Yankees, in 1961 **2.** Babe Didrikson Zaharias (She excelled in basketball, track and field, golf, and tennis.) **3.** Green Bay, Wisconsin **4.** Golf **5.** Polo **6.** Pasadena, California **7.** Cincinnati, Ohio **8.** Althea Gibson **9.** Soccer **10.** Four (He won the 100- and 200-meter dashes, and the broad jump, and was on the winning 400-meter relay team.) **11.** Sailing **12.** Notre Dame **13.** Sports car racing **14.** Hockey **15.** Fencing

What Is It? (page 42)

1. d: A migratory sea bird **2.** k: A large watchdog **3.** c: A furry Australian animal **4.** a: A sticklike insect **5.** h: A species of butterfly **6.** i: A breed of chicken **7.** g: A bat-like marine animal **8.** b: A climbing garden vine **9.** e: A poisonous lizard **10.** j: A Western handgun **11.** f: A professional football player

Who's Zoo? (page 43)

1. Black Sheep **2.** Book Worm **3.** Cheap Skate **4.** Copy Cat **5.**

Dark Horse **6.** Dumb Bunny **7.** Eager Beaver **8.** Early Bird
9. Night Owl **10.** Busy Bee **11.** Lone Wolf **12.** Sitting Duck

Military History (page 44)

1. b: The Battle of Waterloo **2.** c: Francis Marion **3.** b: Benedict
Arnold **4.** c: 1783 (September 3) **5.** a: General Meade **6.** c: Sioux
Indians **7.** a: the Lusitania **8.** a: November 11, 1918 **9.** c: Poland
(on September 1, 1939) **10.** c: Pearl Harbor

For the Birds (page 48)

1. c: Kitty Hawk, North Carolina **2.** c: canary (native to the
Canary Islands) **3.** b: the nightingale **4.** a: The Lone Eagle **5.**
c: square dance callers **6.** b: peacock **7.** a: a griffin **8.** a: Cock
Robin ("I," said the sparrow, "with my bow and arrow, I killed
Cock Robin.") **9.** b: Turkey **10.** b: a famous story by Hans
Christian Andersen (The "ugly duckling" turned out to be a
swan.)

Double Trouble (page 51)

1. tom-tom **2.** Lulu **3.** bon-bon **4.** chow-chow **5.** choo-choo **6.** yo-yo
7. so-so **8.** bye-bye **9.** ma-ma **10.** rah-rah

"Fee, Fi, Fo, Fum!" (page 52)

1. Rumpelstiltskin **2.** "Snow White" **3.** His mother's cow **4.** "The
Emperor's New Clothes" **5.** She let down her hair for him to
climb up. **6.** Tom Thumb, Thumbelina, Thumbkin, Hop O'My
Thumb **7.** Hansel and Gretal **8.** Goldilocks **9.** Puss In Boots
10. Little Red Riding Hood

Ancient and Primitive Man (page 54)

1. a: anthropology **2.** b: the Old Stone Age **3.** c: Japan **4.** b:
the Caribou Eskimos **5.** a: the canoe, sled, skis **6.** b: the Phoenicians

Win, Place or Show (page 56)

1. Animal, Vegetable, and Mineral **2.** Beg, Borrow, or Steal
3. Bell, Book, and Candle **4.** Food, Clothing, and Shelter **5.** Hook,
Line, and Sinker **6.** Liberty, Equality, Fraternity **7.** Morning,
Noon, and Night **8.** Lock, Stock, and Barrel **9.** Masculine,
Feminine, and Neuter **10.** Past, Present, and Future **11.** Stop,
Look, and Listen **12.** Reading, Writing, and Arithmetic **13.** Ready,
Willing, and Able **14.** Length, Width, and Depth (or Breadth)
15. Land, Sea, and Air **16.** Nickel, Dime, and Quarter **17.** Red,

White, and Blue **18.** Blood, Sweat, and Tears **19.** Came, Saw, Conquered **20.** Knife, Fork, and Spoon

Just Say "Ah" (page 58)

1. b: the circulatory system **2.** c: the respiratory system **3.** b: spinal cord **4.** b: in the ear **5.** b: the abdomen **6.** b: white corpuscles **7.** b: in the arm **8.** b: a muscle **9.** a: 98.6°F. **10.** b: 206 **11.** a: 12 pints

Where in the U.S.A.? (page 61)

1. Alaska **2.** Providence **3.** Mount Vernon **4.** Detroit, Michigan **5.** Virginia (Eight presidents were born in this state.) **6.** Akron **7.** North Dakota and South Dakota (The tribe was the Dakotas.) **8.** Lincoln **9.** Plymouth Rock (The Pilgrims landed there in 1620.) **10.** Hawaii

Are You a Good Mixer? (page 63)

1. f: Poet who wrote "The Raven" **2.** e: American bandmaster and composer **3.** g: Author of *Uncle Tom's Cabin* **4.** b: German composer **5.** h: President during World War I **6.** a: Civil war general, later U.S. President **7.** c: American aviator **8.** j: Modern painter, born in Spain **9.** d: Author of "The Star-Spangled Banner" **10.** k: Long-time head of the F.B.I. **11.** i: American scout nicknamed "Buffalo Bill"

The Animal World (page 64)

1. b: American Bison **2.** a: raccoon **3.** b: an oppossum **4.** b: cubs **5.** c: 18 feet **6.** b: a mongoose **7.** a: antelope **8.** a: seal **9.** a: lodges **10.** b: an okapi

Word Search (page 68)

1. Include **2.** Intrude **3.** Insist **4.** Inflate **5.** Inspire **6.** Intend **7.** Induce **8.** Infer **9.** Inform **10.** Intern **11.** Involve **12.** Inspect

What's in a Name? (page 70)

1. a: an apprentice **2.** c: a mill keeper **3.** b: a roofer who uses straw **4.** c: a metal worker **5.** c: a bookkeeper or clerk **6.** c: a gamekeeper or warden **7.** a: a maker of cloth **8.** c: a barrel maker **9.** c: a stone or brick worker **10.** b: a dresser of animal hides

A Capital Quiz (page 73)

1. b: Tokyo **2.** c: Moscow **3.** b: Rome **4.** c: Canberra **5.** c: Ottawa **6.** a: New Delhi **7.** b: Brasilia **8.** a: Madrid **9.** c: Jerusalem **10.** b: Paris